Are You Ready For Summer Camp?

Take this simple test and find out.

1. A duffel bag is:
   (a) a bag that's been badly duffeled.
   (b) a bag for carrying your leftover duffel.
   (c) a combination compass-knife-bait hook-whistle-night-light-and-paper-towel dispenser.
   (d) a bag to carry your combination compass-knife-bait-hook-whistle-night-light-and paper-towel dispenser.

2. If you rub two sticks together for a long time:
   (a) you'll be asked to leave the dance.
   (b) you might miss supper.
   (c) you'll set fire to your duffel bag.
   (d) someone will probably ask you to stop.

3. At camp, the eating area is called the mess hall because:
   (a) it would be confusing to refer to it as the lake.
   (b) no one at camp can spell *cafeteria*.
   (c) after you take one look at it, you won't have to ask!
   (d) it makes it easier to distinguish it from your duffel bag.

If you actually tried to take this test, you need this book more than you think! Keep reading!

**Other Apple® Paperbacks
you will enjoy:**

The Cool Kids' Guide to Summer Camp

Jovial Bob Stine and Jane Stine

Illustrations by Jerry Zimmerman

AN
APPLE®
PAPERBACK

SCHOLASTIC INC.
New York Toronto London Auckland Sydney

*The authors wish to thank
Aram and Noah Salzman for their
camp spirit and invaluable advice.*

ISBN 0-590-40302-8

12 11 10 9 8 7 6 5 4 3 2 1   5   6 7 8 9/8 0 1/9

Printed in the U.S.A.   01

To Rich, the Gremlin

Table of Contents

Test Yourself: Are You Ready for Camp?

Sure, you've packed your digital, glow-in-the-dark canteen, your three-room mobile pup tent, and your combination compass and paper-towel dispenser. But does that mean you're really ready for summer camp?

Take this simple test and find out just how prepared you are.

PART ONE. Choose the best answer for each question.

1. If you rub two sticks together for a long time:
   a) you'll be asked to leave the table.
   b) you'll have skinnier sticks.
   c) someone will probably ask you to stop.

2. At camp, the eating area is called the mess hall because:
   a) it would be confusing to call it the lake.
   b) no one at camp can spell *cafeteria*.
   c) after you take one look at it, you won't have to ask!

PART TWO. In Column A you will find seven popular camp activities. Column B contains equipment used in these activities. Can you match the equipment with the activity it is used in? We've done the first one for you.

Column A

<u>d</u> 1. Dirt diving

___ 2. Fish toss

___ 3. Bunk dousing

___ 4. Food sitting

___ 5. Marshmallow lifts

___ 6. Staring

___ 7. Running away

Column B

a) a thingamabob

b) a thingamajig

c) a something-or-other

d) a stick

e) a stick or two

f) part of a stick

g) yet another stick

PART THREE. Choose one of the topics and write a 2500-word essay on it.

1. How to Wake a Sleeping Bag
2. How to Housebreak a Pup Tent
3. How to Patch up Those Old Swimming Holes

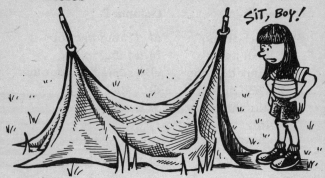

SiT, BOY!

HOW TO SCORE YOURSELF: If you realized there were better things you could be doing than taking this test (such as sleeping or walking around in a daze), you're probably ready for summer camp. If you thought about taking this test—or actually tried to take it—you need this book more than you think. Keep reading!

If you have never been to summer camp before, this book will make you as cool as the longtime, veteran campers. And if you're a longtime, veteran camper, this book will make you as cool as you'd like the first-time campers to think you are!

It's all here: What to expect—and how to deal with the unexpected! What to do—and what to say when you don't know what to do! What to bring. What *not* to bring. And how to get the most out of camp—the most laughs, that is!

Are you really ready for camp?

Don't worry.

After reading this book, you'll be ready for *anything!!*

How to Survive the Older Campers' Friendly Warnings

Congratulations! You are on the bus and on your way to camp. But don't get too comfortable. You are about to face your first big test.

Here comes a group of older campers. They've been to this camp before, and they're ready for you with all kinds of friendly warnings about what to expect. Don't believe them! They're really playing the old camper's favorite game, "Let's Scare the New Camper Half to Death."

You can be ready for them by following this handy guide. We'll show you that what they say is not always what you get! First read what the older campers will tell you about the camp. Then read the real lowdown, the facts.

6

They Say: *"The woods are filled with dangerous animals."*
The Facts: Last year someone spotted two raccoons, a rabbit, and a very nasty-looking chipmunk!

They Say: *"Dozens of kids got hurt last year because they make you ride wild stallions that haven't been broken in!"*
The Facts: Last year Billy fell off old Dobbin when the horse fell asleep.

They Say: *"The camp nurse is really tough. Last year a kid broke his leg, and all she did was put Mercurochrome on it."*
The Facts: Last year a kid broke his leg, and she put a cast on his arm!

They Say: *"The food in the mess hall is terrible."*
The Facts: The food in the mess hall is terrible.

They Say: *"The lake is filled with leeches and jellyfish."*
The Facts: The lake is so muddy, the Loch Ness Monster could be in it and no one would know!

They Say: *"It's too bad you weren't here last summer. This summer can't be nearly as good."*
The Facts: They say this every summer.

They Say: *"Comic books are not allowed. So you'd better let us hide yours."*
The Facts: You have some comics they haven't read yet.

They Say: *"They're really strict about inspection every morning. If your bunk isn't perfectly neat, you get into real trouble."*
The Facts: You pass inspection if the head counselor can get in the cabin door.

They Say: *"You have the meanest counselor in camp. He was kicked out of the marines for being too tough."*
The Facts: Your counselor is a good guy, but last year he yelled at them for stepping on his wildflower collection.

They Say: *"The head counselor drives you crazy by blowing his whistle every minute!"*
The Facts: The head counselor drives you crazy by blowing his whistle every minute!

They Say: *"By the end of summer, everyone has to swim across the lake—and it's over a mile!"*
The Facts: Last summer a few kids tried to swim across the lake and gave up when it started to rain.

They Say: *"All the best kids didn't come back this year."*
The Facts: They say this every year.

They Say: *"The mosquitoes at this camp are as big as bats!"*
The Facts: The mosquitoes at this camp are as big as bats!

They Say: *"Oh, you're in Bunk 10. I hope they got rid of the bats!"*
The Facts: They weren't bats—they were mosquitoes.

They Say: *"I hope you know all the words to the camp alma mater. If not, they make you stand in front of the whole camp and sing it solo."*
The Facts: Not even the camp owner knows the words to the camp alma mater!

They Say: *"I hope your trunk arrived okay. Last year Jennie's trunk never came, and* she had to wear one pair of shorts all summer."

The Facts: Everyone wears one pair of shorts all summer!

Okay, now you're ready for them. You know the facts behind their scariest stories. You can sit back, enjoy the bus ride, and think about how much fun you'll have scaring the new campers next year!

How to Look Like a Cool Camper

If you want to be a cool camper, you've got to look like one. That doesn't mean you have to rush out and buy a trunkful of new clothes and gear. In fact, *new* is the last thing you want.

To look like a cool camper, you have to look like the kind of kid who's been going to camp since he was three. So *what* if you're a first-timer and the closest you ever came to a camp was the time you visited your little sister at day camp! It's really easy to perfect the cool camper's look.

Take a look at these diagrams. Diagram A shows your typical first-time camper. Diagram B shows the old-timer.

Got the picture?

New Camper

Tennis racket

Haircut that's short enough to last all summer

Dark glasses to protect eyes from bright sun

Book of camp songs for campfires

Sparkling clean official camp T-shirt

Eager grin

Bright-colored shirt so he can be seen and won't be lost in the woods

Nose clips for diving

Name tapes everywhere to make sure he gets all his clothes back from the laundry

Life-preserving kit: compass, 10-bladed knife, canteen, flint, first-aid kit

Baggy new camp shorts so he can grow into them

Flashlight for night survival

Clean white socks

Brand-new shiny hiking boots

Backpack containing all equipment needed for overnight hike

Old Camper

Baseball cap to cover haircut he got last summer which was short enough to last all last summer, this winter, and next summer

Someone else's name tape because you never get your own clothes back from the laundry

Dark glasses so no one can tell he's asleep when the head counselor is giving a speech

Knowing grin

Ratty old T-shirt worn inside out to look as if he doesn't care what he looks like

Greenish-brown shirt so he won't be noticed when the counselor is looking for volunteers

Nose clips for mess hall food

Flyswatter

Flashlight for reading after taps

Transistor radio for drowning out camp songs

Life-preserving kit: roll of dimes for phone and candy machines

Same old camp shorts from last year—another 3 summers and they'll be tight enough

Pink socks (everything comes back from the laundry pink)

Backpack for hiding comic books, magazines, gum, potato chips, candy bars, and toilet paper

Brand-new-looking hiking boots (hiking boots don't wear out if the farthest you walk is from the bunk to the mess hall)

A Guided Tour

That first day of camp, you're going to be really busy—busy trying to figure out where to put the life-sized photo of your dog that you couldn't bear to part with, and where to hide the fuzzy pink pajamas with feet your mother forced you to bring!

You probably won't even have time to look around. That's why we've prepared this exclusive guided tour for you. Now you can tour your camp before you even get there.

Take our guided tour—please. Then, when everyone else is wandering around in circles trying to find the Rec Hall, you won't be able to find it either—but at least you can explain to them what it is they can't find!

THE BUNK

No, that's not the shed where they keep the garbage trucks. That's your bunk.

What were you expecting—a Holiday Inn?

The bunk is a good place to begin our tour because you'll want to get here right away to choose your bed. As you can see, all of the beds look pretty much alike. They all look like torture racks from an old Vincent Price movie. Rule Number One in deciding which bed to claim is: Try not to choose any of the ones with three legs!

But don't let their appearance fool you.

Just sleep in yours for one night.

The next morning you will discover the truth about camp beds—they are a true scientific marvel. No matter how hard you try, you can't get out of them in the morning!

Let's move on around the room. Those small gray objects along the floor? Those are called dust kitties. Don't worry—you'll find out about them soon enough. In fact, you'll spend about half your time in the bunk sweeping them up! (Who said you wouldn't discover new forms of wildlife here at camp?)

That chart posted on the wall next to the boarded-up window is the bunk duty roster. It assigns everyone in the bunk a lot of strange jobs that have to do with cleaning.

You'll want to get out of doing your assigned job whenever possible. The best way to do this is to come prepared with your own list of jobs that you would prefer to do. Here are some jobs you might volunteer for:

1. Mattress Endurance Tester
2. Comic Book Duplication Inspector
3. Pillow Fluffer
4. Sunburn Peeling Coordinator
5. Tissue Folder

Now, step over those dust kitties and we'll move on to our next stop on this tour.

THE MESS HALL

A lot of fun things happen in the mess hall, but perhaps the most popular entertainment here is Plate Dropping. Whenever some poor kid drops his lunch or dinner plate, the whole place goes crazy with everyone clapping, cheering, and laughing. See? It's just like at home!

Of course, the food isn't exactly like the food back home. In fact, it isn't exactly like the food on Earth!

But like every dining establishment, the mess hall has its specialties of the house. Here are some of the delicacies you will soon be enjoying, items which can be found only in camp mess halls:

1. Hot chocolate with a unique elastic skin on the top. We don't know how they get that thick skin on top of the hot chocolate—and we really don't *want* to know. You can lift it off with a fork and use it as a Frisbee. Or you can try to pull it apart with your bare hands—but few kids are strong enough! At one camp we visited, the kids decided to see if they could stretch the skin from their hot chocolate across an entire table. (The kids at your camp are probably a lot more sophisticated.)

2. Did you ever wonder what happens to the leftover papier-maché from Arts & Crafts? Try the mess hall's hot cereal in the morning and you'll wonder no more! Camp hot cereal sticks to your ribs—and to your spoon, the bowl, and the floor! The other unique thing about the hot cereal

served here is that it's almost always ice-cold!

3. Mystery meat stew is a mess hall tradition. It's also one mystery you won't want to get to the bottom of!

4. The chocolate pudding served at camp has the same elastic skin floating on top as the hot chocolate. How do they do that?!?

THE REC HALL

As you can see, it has started to rain a little. It's just a drizzle—probably won't amount to more than three or four inches.

Let's go inside and we'll show you—hey, watch out for that puddle!

Ha ha. That was a deep one, wasn't it!

You've got to watch out for those deep ones. Don't worry, those clothes'll dry off by August.

The Rec Hall is where you'll be spending a lot of time when it rains. What do you do here? Well, you'll mainly wait for the rain to stop.

There's a lot of recreational equipment in here for campers. If they ever find the net, you'll be able to play Ping-Pong on that table over there.

The Rec Hall is also where the Camp Show is staged. If you're interested in serious, high-quality theater, you might want to run away right now. If you stick around, you'll learn that this year they're staging a musical version of the multiplication tables written by the drama counselor's six-year-old niece. It's supposed to have some great numbers!

THE ARTS & CRAFTS CENTER

Through this door over here is the Arts & Crafts Center. Those paintings on the walls and that beadwork in the display cases were all done by last year's campers. For some reason, they all chose to donate their work to the camp rather than bring it home with them!

You may have heard that there's no variety in Arts & Crafts at camp, that you have to make the same old things that everyone else always has to make. Well,

beads
beaded belts
beaded wallets
beaded strings
belted beads
beaded beads
belted beaded wallets
beaded wallet belts
stringed wallets
string ties
beaded ties
tied beads
belted beaded ties
beaded tie belts
belted tie beads
beaded dust kitties

that just isn't true. Here is a list of only a *few* of the wide variety of projects you can do in Arts & Crafts.

THE WATERFRONT

Yes, the lake is really beautiful, isn't it? And, as you can see, the camp does have all the equipment that was promised in the brochure—water skis, motorboats, canoes, and sailboats. It's all so much fun! Just ask the counselors, who spend all the time using the equipment while you watch from shore!

Don't be fooled by those waterfront counselors over there wearing sweatshirts and thermal underwear. The water is really warm—at least it will be once you get used to it—around August 18th!

Still, everyone knows that once you get in the water, you just won't want to come out. To help you stay in the water when all the counselors are blowing their whistles and trying to drag you out, here are some handy lines you might try:

1. "No, I haven't been in too long. My face turns blue, my teeth chatter, and my skin wrinkles up like a prune *whenever* I'm having a good time!"

2. "I'm just being generous and giving everyone else a chance to shower and get to the mess hall first. Really. I don't care

if I miss the first course of mystery meat paste on a stick!"

3. "It's Daylight Savings Time, isn't it? That means I get another hour!"

THE INFIRMARY

That's the infirmary over there, the clean building. Don't worry about it. You won't have to go there. You're not getting out of going on the five-mile hike *that* easily!

THE SPORTS FIELD

Yes, the baseball diamond is really impressive. A lot of scientists from all over the country are impressed with it, too. They're interested in a scientific fact that's true of all summer camp baseball fields: No matter where you stand on the field, no matter what position you play, and no matter what time of day you play, you'll always have the sun right in your face. Amazing, isn't it?

THE CAMPFIRE

Well, here's the last stop on our guided tour. This is a good place to stop because it's probably the place you'll remember most.

Next winter when you're fighting to keep your head above the snowdrifts, when the freezing wind blows your hat off and whips it under the wheels of a passing truck, when you fall headfirst into a puddle of freezing brown water, when you're sneezing and coughing and hacking and wheezing—you'll think back to the campfire. You'll think back to this spot here.

The jokes, the stories, the games, the songs.

You won't remember any of those.

But you'll remember the crisp, tangy taste of that first barbecued hot dog, the mustard dripping off the charcoal-toasted roll. And the perfect marshmallows, hot and black outside, soft and sweet on the inside, melting on your tongue.

Forget the songs and the silly games!

The cool camper knows that the incredible outdoor food is what the campfire is all about.

You'll remember the taste of the—hey—stop that!

Stop drooling like that!

This is only an imaginary tour—remember!

The Cool Kids' Guide to Campers:

Ten Kids You Won't Be Able to Avoid This Summer

Let's face it. Not every kid can be as sweet, as charming, as cool and adorable as you. Even the best camp has its share of campers you could easily live without.

The funny thing is, it doesn't matter if you're at a wilderness survival camp, an underwater singing camp, or a tag-team wrestling camp. The same kids seem to show up everywhere! For example, there's—

THE OLD-TIMER

She remembers the camp "when it was good." In other words, before "new kids" (translation: you) got there. Her favorite expression is, "If you think this is fun, that's because you weren't here three years ago!"

But if you can put up with her constant reminders of how much clearer the lake used to be, how much cooler the kids were, and how much nicer the counselors were, the Old-Timer is a useful person to have around—mainly because she knows all the gossip about everyone!

THE PRINCE

You can recognize the Prince at any camp—he's the one with the chauffeur-driven canoe and the monogrammed pup tent. His idea of a hike is when the car lets him off at the end of the driveway instead of bringing him to his door.

All in all, the Prince is not a bad kid to have in your bunk—especially if he shares his food packages from home. You'll be amazed at how fast you can develop a taste for caviar and pâté de foie gras when the alternative is mess hall mystery meatloaf!

THE COUNSELOR'S PET

You can usually find the Counselor's Pet at the equipment shed, cheerfully stacking the croquet wickets or canoe paddles. She always wears a camp T-shirt—not just on Visiting Day. And her favorite expression is: "Bunk Spirit!"

The Counselor's Pet is not a bad bunkmate. You can usually get her to make your bed so that it will look "shipshape." But be careful—Counselor's Pets have been known to wake up *before* reveille and make your bed while you're still in it!

THE HOMESICK KID

Actually, you won't see too much of this kid. He spends most of his time calling home or writing letters. His red-rimmed eyes and shaky voice might really get you down—if you didn't know that this is the fifth summer in a row that he's pulled this same scene!

THE EXPERT

"That's not the way to open your trunk. Watch how I do it!"

If those are the first words a kid says to you, you may be in the presence of the Expert. He's a kid ready to give you advice on every subject—whether you want it or not.

Gymnastics? He taught Kurt Thomas.

Hiking? "This is nothing. Now, Mt. McKinley—that's a hill!"

Our expert advice for dealing with this kid—stay underwater as much as possible!

MR. COMPETITION

He's *got* to be the first and the best at
everything! By the third day of camp, he's
already beaten all of the kids and half of
the counselors at arm wrestling. He's the
sort of kid who wants to count your mosquito bites to make sure you don't have
more than he does!

THE PRANKSTER

He's the one who constantly tells tales of great pranks and practical jokes he pulled at his other camp. If he had really done all that he claims, he'd be on the FBI's Ten Most Wanted List! His tall tales eventually get to be such a bore that he's the only kid in camp to have his bed short-sheeted! And he's the only kid who will fall for the old toothpaste-in-the-shoes trick!

THE COMPLAINER

She puts *everything* down. She mopes around all summer, complains about everything and everyone, and somehow manages to avoid doing anything that's fun.

Then on the last day of camp you'll find her crying her eyes out, saying that it's been the best summer of her life and she can't wait for camp to start again next year!

THE SHRINKING VIOLET

The Shrinking Violet is a little timid about camp. In fact, ever since she saw a "wild animal" outside the mess hall, she's given up eating. (She just won't believe that chipmunks don't bite!)

Of course she's excused from swimming in the lake. She's allergic to any water that doesn't come in a bottle!

THE SINGER

She's the one who never misses an opportunity to start "Found A Peanut" or some other endless, boring song. Of course she can't carry a tune. But most annoying of all is the fact that she interrupts each of the ninety-nine choruses to exclaim, "Come on, guys—eveyone join in now!"

The last chapter helped get you ready for your fellow campers. Now, it's time to prepare for those wild and crazy counselors. Here is—

The Cool Kids' Guide to Counselors:

Nine Counselors You'll Find at Every Camp

THE NEATNESS FANATIC

It's a dark day in camp when it's her turn to inspect the bunks. She'll take away points if your mosquito bites aren't lined up!

She's so thorough, she checks inside your pillow for dust!

Talk about neat! Before she'll let you build a fire, she washes all the firewood!

THE SNAKE LOVER

He's the nature counselor—but his main purpose in life is to convince the world that giant boa constrictors can be cuddly. By the end of summer, most campers are still not convinced. However, everyone agrees that watching the python swallow a whole mouse is a lot more entertaining than most of the camp movies!

The Snake Lover's favorite expression is, "Snakes aren't slimy, you know"—and he's right—they're not, but *he is!*

THE MODEL

Every camp has one. A counselor who is simply beautiful—and being beautiful is her whole job!

Of course she takes this job very seriously. Her instruction periods on hair-combing and nail-polish-removing are the best attended at camp—especially by the male counselors!

What sport is she in charge of? No one can say for sure. The only equipment anyone sees her carry is her hair dryer!

THE DRILL SERGEANT

Someone should explain to the Drill Sergeant that this is a summer camp—not a marine boot camp! He spends all his time barking orders, trying to keep kids in line, and giving stern pep talks.

He's so strict, he won't let the moon shine after lights-out! He's so tough, he roasts marshmallows in his hand!

At most camps, he's the head waterfront counselor. But watch out! You know you've gone to a really tough camp when the Drill Sergeant is the Arts & Crafts counselor!

THE INVISIBLE COUNSELOR

Every camp has one, but you've got to look fast to see him. He's usually around for the first day or two, and he sometimes shows up for meals. But the rest of the time, he uses his amazing power to become invisible.

Need a counselor for lifeguard duty? He has disappeared!

Ready for the five-mile hike? He's gone!

Of course, he's also invisible when you're reading after taps, sneaking extra snacks, and talking during rest period. No doubt about it—in some ways the Invisible Counselor is the best counselor of all!

THE WHISTLE BLOWER

This important job is usually held by the head counselor. In the mess hall, at the flag pole, and on the baseball fields, his lungs could qualify him for the Olympic Eardrum Shattering Team! Of course, he really comes into his own at the water-front, where the sound of his whistle really carries—like to Saudi Arabia and back!

Not much else is known about Whistle Blowers. They don't take the whistles out of their mouths long enough to have a conversation. Besides, due to their long-winded whistle-blowing, most of them are just about stone deaf!

THE BIG-TIME OPERATOR

The head counselor may think he runs the camp, but cool campers soon learn that the Big-Time Operator is really the man in charge. One look around his bunk and you'll agree: wall-to-wall carpet on the floor, easy chairs, and an air-conditioner.

He's so slick he can convince first-time counselors that they need to buy tickets to the lake—and tickets to *get out* of the lake! The Big-Time Operator even knows the best-kept secret at camp—where they keep the Ping-Pong paddles!

THE JOKER

"Didja hear the one about. . . ."

"This'll crack you up!"

"What do you get when you cross. . . ."

Beware of any counselor who comes up to you with phrases like these. You may be in the presence of one of the most common camp pests—the Joker.

The Joker goes through the twenty jokes he knows by the second day of camp. Then he starts all over again. Strangely enough, the jokes don't get any funnier the eighth time you've heard them!

Be especially careful to avoid him when you have a sunburn. This is because nine times out of ten, the Joker is also a Backslapper!

THE GREAT DIRECTOR

So *what* if your camp show is a less classy version of *The Gong Show?* The drama counselor acts as if it's "next stop—Broadway!" Rushing around, calling everyone "dahling," the drama counselor never leaves the Rec Hall—or, as she insists on calling it, "my theater!"

The drama counselor is always bragging about all the big stars she's worked with on Broadway. And it is true that someone did see her once in a TV commercial—with Lassie!

We Interrupt the Cool Kids' Guide to Summer Camp for These Important Sunburn Prevention Tips!

(From the Office of the Coordinator of the Director of the Information Officer of the Department Head of the Guy Who Makes Up Tips from the National Sunburn Prevention Center for the Prevention of Sunburn and the Production of Tips on Sunburn Protection and the Direction of Information on Preventing Misinformation about the Prevention of Sunburn Information Center.)

1. Stand as far away from the sun as possible.
2. Sunbathe at night whenever weather permits.
3. Keep your back to the sun whenever possible.

The Cool Kids' Guide to Observing Wildlife

Just how wild is the wildlife you will find at camp?

Fortunately, the answer to that question is: *not* as wild as the other campers say!

In their desire to make sure you have an exciting summer older campers may exaggerate a bit about the kinds of animal life the camp has to offer. Yes, you all hear those crunching sounds right outside the window. But the animal doing the crunching may not be as interesting as your fellow campers would like you to believe.

Keep this convenient chapter with you. It will help you keep a realistic view of the wildlife in and around your camp.

THE MOST COMMON WILDLIFE

Kids who are eager to become wildlife observers should begin with the most common form of camp wildlife—the old horse. Summer camps are a natural habitat for old horses, and your camp is bound to have at least a few. (To observe dozens of old horses, you have to go to a riding camp!)

Old horses are easy to observe and easy to find. Just follow your nose!

You do not have to sneak up on old horses to observe them. They are usually grateful for any attention. If you like to photograph wildlife, old horses make the perfect subjects since they seldom move.

It's perfectly safe to pet old horses, and even safer to ride them. That's because no matter how much you yell, nudge, kick, and urge them on, they will walk along at a slow, safe speed of their own choosing. And don't worry about falling off. Most old horses come with backs that slope down so low your feet touch the ground as you ride!

OTHER LARGE ANIMALS OF THE WILD

Many summer camps are located near farms. This gives the eager wildlife observer a chance to stalk even larger prey—the cow. Cows have many of the same qualities as old horses, yet few campers make any attempt at all to observe them.

In a survey of dozens of campers who agreed to talk to us (if we didn't use their names or tell anyone they talked to us), we asked the following question: Why don't you want to observe cows as part of your wildlife studies? When the kids stopped laughing, we received these answers:

They all look alike	45%
They're boring	22%
They're not interesting	20%
They have no personality	13%
All they do is eat grass	10%
They're extremely boring	8%
They're most certainly extremely boring	4%
Please go away	2%
Undecided	2%

When we totaled up the answers, we were astonished to find that they added up to 126%—which indicates to us that even *more* campers than we talked to are not at all interested in observing cows. Either that, or there's something dreadfully wrong with this survey!

SMALLER CREATURES

All summer camps abound with smaller forms of wildlife. Before you realize it, you may find yourself observing gnats. No one really knows where gnats come from. But everyone knows where they hang out— around your campfire when you're trying to eat dinner!

Gnats are not colorful. In fact, they are rather drab. They don't have interesting faces. And their personalities leave a lot to be desired. Yet they make up for these faults by being extremely attentive. Once gnats have found you, they seldom leave you alone!

Gnats are easy to observe—mainly because they never travel in groups of less than 50,000! Studying gnats is also convenient since you never have to come to them—they come to you!

Many a campfire rings out with the sound of busy campers slapping at gnats far into the night. Most any camper will admit that camp just wouldn't be the same without them!

LAKE MONSTERS

You're swimming quietly in the lake, minding your own business, when suddenly something unbelievably yucky grabs your big toe, sending you leaping two feet out of the water. You have just encountered one of the most common species of camp wildlife—the lake monster.

Lake monsters live underwater in every lake that is near a summer camp. Lake monsters don't really harm anyone. They just like to grab campers' toes to give them a little thrill.

From campers' descriptions, we know

that they range in size from one mile long to fifty miles long. Yet they are so fast that no one has ever seen one!

WHAT ABOUT BEARS?

Every summer camp is filled with talk about bears, especially if it is located near a forest, a woods, or a few shrubs. At your camp, lots of kids will think they hear bears at night. You'll search the woods with flashlights. You'll spend hours peering out into the darkness. You'll listen for the footsteps and low growls.

But you will never see a bear.

Not one.

The entire summer.

That's because summer camps everywhere are populated only by invisible bears.

Invisible bears make all the noises that regular bears make. You'll hear them prowling around the garbage cans and rattling the door of the equipment shed. Sometimes you'll hear them walking brazenly right up to your bunk door. But for some reason that even scientists can't (or won't) explain, these bears never leave any footprints.

A lot of campers become disappointed when they cannot see the bears they know they hear. But, you'll have to admit, invisible bears are better than no bears at all!

Cool Camper's Exercise Program

MORNING

1. One deep knee bend.
2. Now see if the other knee will bend.
3. One elbow bend.
4. If elbow bends, use it to pull covers up over your head.

NIGHT

1. One sit-up. (Since you are bound to be tired, begin in a sitting position.)
2. One hand-lift to mouth. (Good for covering up yawns.)
3. On count of three, lower head to pillow.
4. Hey, wake up—there are more exercises.
5. Come on, wake up! We're not finished!

The Cool Kids' Guide to REAL Camp Sports

Baseball? Swimming? Horseback riding? Oh, sure, a lot of kids spend some time in the summer playing around with these sports. But those aren't the sports that really *involve* everyone. After reading this chapter, you'll be prepared for the *real* sports that all campers play.

GOSSIPING ABOUT COUNSELORS

Most sports take only a few hours to play, but you'll soon discover that *this* sport takes the entire summer! A counselor who shows up five minutes late for breakfast can get an entire bunk going at this sport for hours, while a counselor's single sheepish grin can throw the game into extra innings and keep an entire camp buzzing for days.

"Who is he going out with?"

"What does she do in real life?"

"Why is he smiling at her like that?"

"Why is she wearing *that* sweater?"

"Who sends him all those letters?"

The questions in this sport never change. But luckily, you've got all summer to dream up really interesting answers!

FOOD GOBBLING

Many new campers are surprised and confused when they see other campers grabbing their stomachs, doubling over, and groaning in agony. These new campers don't realize that their bunkmates have been playing a popular camp sport—food gobbling.

Everyone knows the dangers of this sport—especially when beef goulash is on the mess hall menu. But after a hard day of gossiping about the counselors, everyone has such a ravenous appetite that it's impossible to resist another round of this fast-moving, two-handed sport.

While the mess hall is a good place to practice food gobbling, the sport doesn't really get under way until a food package from home arrives. Then, what is usually

an individual sport quickly becomes a team sport as everyone in the bunk tries his or her hand at gobbling up everything in the package!

HIDING YOUR STUFF

This challenging sport cannot be tried until you have mastered the sport of bed-making. Its rules are actually quite simple: You try to hide all the stuff you were supposed to put away *inside the bed* without anyone noticing that your bed is a bit lumpier than it should be! Many new campers should not even attempt this sport since it requires patience, skill, and the ability to squeeze everything you own into the shape of a pillow!

BRAGGING

Here's a creative, imaginative sport that's a favorite of many campers. The game is easy to learn—you simply brag about anything that comes to mind.

Most campers brag about their home, about their parents' cars, about their pets, or their school. However, those who really know this sport spend most of their time bragging about the camp they went to last year, which was much better in every way than the camp you're at this year!

This sport can be more difficult than it

sounds. That's because more and more campers are eager to play yet another sport—*bragger-punching!*

HIDING AND SWAPPING COMIC BOOKS

While many campers pretend to be inter-ested in swimming, exercise, and Arts & Crafts, the truth is that just about every-one comes to camp for the purpose of reading, swapping, and sneaking comic books. Most serious campers arrive ready to play this sport, with a stack of at least twenty comic books hidden in a secret compartment in the trunk. The rules of the sport call for the player not only to keep his comic books from being lost, stolen, or confiscated, but to read everyone else's comics, usually at times when comic books are not allowed to be read.

Yes, it's a dangerous sport. But most campers seriously believe it's well worth the effort. The secret of the sport is, of course, to be quick, to be sneaky, to be able to read by flashlight inside a sleep-ing bag—and to stay away from the misguided camper who brought his back issues of *Humpty Dumpty* to camp!

SCRATCHING

Yes, of course this is a popular camp sport. But do we have to discuss it here?!?

SUNBURN PEELING

This sport is an individual rather than a team sport, and it's a popular after-taps activity. Sunburn peeling is often played simultaneously with another camp sport—scratching. But we're still determined not to discuss that here!

TOWEL SNAPPING

For many camp athletes, there's no more satisfying moment in sports than the sound of a towel snapping against someone's bare body when they've just stepped out of the shower or are dressing to go swimming. The THWACK of snapping towels can be heard in summer camps across the nation, followed by hearty cries of pain.

Although it's very popular, we don't recommend this sport—mainly because it's traditional for every *snapper* to immediately become a *snappee*. Ouch!

GETTING AND RETURNING EQUIPMENT

So you think canoeing is a challenge? It's not half as challenging as the sport of checking out the canoe and then checking it back in when you're finished!

Archery may appeal to a lot of campers as a fun way to pass the time. But you'll pass a lot more time and get a lot more exercise going through the lengthy procedure of checking out the bows and arrows and targets!

Our surveys show that most campers spend so much time playing the sport of checking in and checking out equipment, they barely have enough time for another popular camp sport—*complaining* about how much time it takes to check out and check in equipment!

BED-MAKING

This difficult physical sport requires more practice than most. But don't worry—you'll getting plenty of it! A recent survey of 100 typical summer camps (including Camp Typical) showed that campers spend an average of 50 percent of their time making their beds, another 50 percent of their time unmaking their beds, and another 50 percent listening to instructions on how to make their beds!

HIDING

A perennial favorite among new campers and old, this sport is popular mainly as a way to avoid gossiping, food gobbling, bed-making, scratching, and all the other hideous activities described in this chapter!

Are you starting to wonder what's going on back home? Do you find yourself thinking about your clean room, your soft bed, home-cooked meals? Well, STOP RIGHT THERE!! You won't be homesick for long once you start remembering the way it *really* is at home. And we'll help you remember with this—

Guaranteed Homesickness Cure

HOW CAN YOU BE HOMESICK WHEN YOU KNOW THAT BACK HOME—

The swimming pool is so crowded, they had to invent a new stroke called the "Sardine"!

Your little brother is so bored, he's been asking if he could mow the lawn a day early!

The same movie has been playing at your neighborhood theater for eight weeks—and you saw it before you left.

The most exciting thing that happens is when the ice-cream truck comes half an hour early!

You'd be sharing your room with your visiting Aunt Martha who snores!

The only thing you haven't already seen on TV at least twice is a series called "You and the Metric System"!

The only kid who didn't go away this summer is Murray, who spends hours and hours talking about his milk-carton collection!

It's so hot that you could fry an egg on the sidewalk—and the kids are so bored that they're trying it!

Your family always arrives at the beach at the same time as the jellyfish!

You'd be stuck again in the backseat with the dog when the family goes on its weekly twelve-hour drive to the country.

You'd have to go to sleep when it was still light out.

The main activity is talking about how you wish you'd gone to camp this summer!

Don't tell us—our homesickness cure wasn't enough? You still find yourself thinking about the gang back home? Okay—try this. If you were home, what would you be doing all day? That's right— you'd be stuck watching daytime TV shows, the soaps, the games, the sitcoms you usually sit and stare at all summer long!

Tell you what we're going to do. We're going to bring the TV out to you so you can catch up with those daytime shows. If this doesn't cure you, you're not homesick —you're just plain sick!

What You Missed Today on Daytime TV

"**The Newlywed Fistfight Game.**" Emily and Jonathan Wallhugger, the cute young couple from Whereshee Falls, won a trip to France by beating Sally and Lemuel Franklinmint to a pulp before the buzzer went off. But in the Grand Fistfight Finale, the Wallhuggers were disqualified when he tore the sleeve off her dress and she failed to give him a bloody nose.

"The Young and the Silly." Marsha broke her engagement to John when she discovered that he likes his toast black. Jillian finally got up the courage to tell her parakeet that he's adopted. Henrietta refused to forgive Sam for chewing on aluminum foil in front of her mother. Jillian broke up with Murray because he couldn't stop winking, and Ellen made the painful decision to sue her dog for defamation of character, slander, and getting mud on the couch.

"Pass the Turtle!" Couple Number Three passed the turtle continuously for three days and became eligible for the Giant Tortoise Toss. Couple Number Four were not so lucky. They dropped the turtle on their second try and had to clean up the mess.

"Love of Cheese." Wainright began to suspect that people have been dropping letters on his head because he's been accidentally living in the mailbox instead of his apartment. Willy claimed that he was nowhere near the marshmallow factory on the night of the fire, but Police Lieutenant Godfrey questioned him about the white food stains all over his face.

"Guess What!" Mystery Panelist Number Three turned out to be a complete mystery to everyone—a stranger who wandered in off the street and thought he was in a used-bread store. Contestant Number Two asked to have the rules explained to her, which stopped the game for the rest of the week. No one could guess the exact price of the new car, and so it was smashed to bits with a wood mallet.

"My, Oh My, That's Mitzi!" Mitzi didn't want Harry to discover that she accidentally stuffed the turkey with his best sports jacket, so she dressed up as a rooster and decided to tell Harry they were invited to a costume party. When Harry unexpectedly brought the boss home for dinner, Mitzi hid on the cocktail table, hoping to be mistaken for a bowl of cheese dip. And then the fun began!

We Interrupt
the Cool Kids' Guide
to Summer Camp
for These Important—

Wildlife Survival Tips!

(From the Coordinating Coordinator of the Corporate Coordination Planning Board of Coordinating Planning Boards of Corporate Planning Coordinates of Planning Coordination for the Survival of Wildlife Tips for the Survival of Wildlife Coordination Bureau Planning Board of Wildlife Survival and Survival Tips.)

1. Don't tease a charging rhinoceros.
2. Don't attempt to photograph the molars of a hungry bear.
3. Do not step on anything that's green and gooey and has eyes and lips—if possible.

You Know
You Won't Enjoy
the Social When—

You think you're ready for the big social.
You've decided exactly what to wear (if
you can only get the grass stains out),
what to do with your hair (if it will only
grow out by Friday), and how to improve
your dancing (don't trip so often).

Chances are, you're going to have a
great time. But be careful—these evenings
don't always go as planned. Just to be on
the safe side, cool campers should keep in
mind these friendly warnings—

Everyone in camp borrows your clothes, so you have nothing left to wear but the shorts you had on the five-mile hike and an old T-shirt that says "Happy Tykes Day Camp"!

Your bunkmate convinces you to spend six hours letting her give you a brand-new hairdo. Then when you get to the social, everyone asks if you just fell in the lake!

It's a come-as-you-are social, and you're wearing a wet bathing suit and flippers!

The counselor in charge insists that everyone learn the dance that all the kids do where he comes from. So, as soon as you arrive, you're given wooden shoes, ten-foot stilts, and a sheep!

Everyone makes fun of your wild dancing when you're actually just scratching your mosquito bites!

The camp's only record player breaks, and you have to take turns humming so that people can dance!

You're finally dancing a romantic, slow dance with the girl you like, and someone changes the record to "The Mexican Hat Dance"!

There's a mix-up with the boys' camp that's coming to your social, and all the boys they send are five years younger than you and think they've come for pony rides!

You've figured out all kinds of clever things you want to say to the boy you really like, but he only wants to talk about how funny it was when you sat down in grape soda!

A Complete Letter-Writing Guide

Forget about "Having a wonderful time— wish you were here!" Now you can drop those boring clichés and write fascinating letters—in the time it takes the other campers to sharpen their pencils.

Here is a list of *every phrase you'll* ever *need*—anything you might ever want to say in a letter home. Go through the list, pick out seven or eight good phrases, and put them together into an entertaining—and informative—letter home.

Hi, everyone,

A. Having an exciting time at camp!
Having a surprising time at camp!
Having a most unusual time at camp!
Having quite a time of it at camp!

B. Hope you got my last letter.
Hope you didn't take my last letter seriously.
Please ignore my last letter and my next letter.
I'll explain everything when I get home.

C. My trunk arrived in good shape.
My trunk arrived in good shape, but I haven't been able to open it.
My trunk arrived, but at the wrong camp.
My trunk arrived, but it was empty.
My trunk arrived, and I'm living in it since there aren't enough bunks.
My trunk hasn't arrived yet, but I'm not worried since it's only been five weeks.

My trunk was lost in the flood, but so
was everyone else's.
I'll explain when I get home.

D. The other kids in my bunk are great.
The other kids in my bunk are
interesting.
The other kids in my bunk are a real
far-out experience.
The other kids in my bunk are missing.
I'll explain when I get home.

E. I'm learning a lot about wildlife here.
I'm learning a lot about life in the wild
here.
I'm learning a lot of wild things here.
I'm learning a lot about survival—especially since all the counselors de-
serted last week.

F. The lake is everything they said it
would be.
The lake is everything they said it
would be—and lots more!
They're cleaning the lake, so I'm sure
what happened yesterday won't
happen again.
I'll explain when I get home.

G. The food in the mess hall is
indescribable.
The food in the mess hall is beyond
description.

The food in the mess hall is beyond belief.

I don't want to say that the food isn't fresh, but the egg salad had feathers in it!

Several horses disappeared from the stable on the day before they served meatloaf.

Please send food!

H. Horseback riding is a real thrill.

Horseback riding is a real thrill, but it would be more thrilling if the horse was alive.

Horseback riding is a real thrill—even on a cow.

Horseback riding is a real thrill—at least that's what the counselors who get to do it say.

The horses seem a lot calmer today, so what happened yesterday probably won't happen again.

I'll explain when I get home.

I. My tennis game is really improving—especially since they've let me use a racket.

My tennis game is really improving—and it's so much more challenging to play it on sand.

I'm afraid I won't be playing much more tennis this summer—someone lost the camp tennis ball.

J. Did you know that gangrene can't be cured?

I'll explain when I get home.

I'm scratching a lot less now. A lot less than some kids around here!

K. We're going on an overnight hike as soon as the counselors can raise bail.

We're going on an overnight hike as soon as we dig out.

We're going on an overnight hike as soon as the quarantine is lifted.

We're going on an overnight hike as soon as we figure out where we are now.

L. Last night we roasted marshmallows in the campfire.

Last night we roasted something in the campfire.

I always learn a lot around the campfire.

Last night I learned why it's not smart to sit too close to the campfire.

Please send me new sneakers!

M. Sorry I can't write more often, but they
only force us to write once a month!
I'd write more often, but you wouldn't
believe it anyway.
I'd write more often, but we have to
use the stationery for towels.
I'll explain when I get home.
Please send food!

The Cool Camper's Instant Letter to a Friend

Even with our handy list, letter-writing can be hard work. After all, you do have to write actual words. Here's a way to avoid all that. With our Cool Camper's Instant Letter, all you do is fill in the blanks, check the right boxes, and mail it off!

Dear _____,

I'm having a fabulous time at Camp
_____. I just couldn't wait
to write and tell you all about it.

The bus ride was really an experience.
The most exciting part was:
☐ when I discovered I was on the
wrong bus to the wrong camp.
☐ pushing the bus twelve miles so the
driver could save gasoline.
☐ getting carsick.
☐ finally arriving after no rest stops
for 500 miles.

When we first pulled in, I couldn't be
lieve it! I wondered:
☐ why they had changed the name of
the camp to CONDEMNED.
☐ how they ever built all those cabins
on quicksand.
☐ why the bus driver let us off without stopping the bus.
☐ why the head counselor was wearing a combat helmet.

All the other campers were just as excited as I was. The first thing they
wanted to do was:
☐ turn around and go home.
☐ get vaccinated against swamp fever.
☐ ask the head counselor why he was
wearing a combat helmet.
☐ write their congressman.

My bunkmates are very nice. We spend
most of our time:

☐ swapping flashlight batteries.
☐ starting campfires in our cabin.
☐ making collect calls to Yugoslavia.
☐ burying our dirty clothes in the woods.

Diving into a real lake for the first
time was exciting. It was also educa-
tional because:

☐ the lake is only three inches deep.
☐ I never knew that water can clot.
☐ I had never been that close to a pir-
anha before.
☐ I got a chance to see how mouth-to-
mouth resuscitation works.

The food here is not at all like the food
at home. For one thing:

☐ it's furry.
☐ I've never seen gray Jell-o.
☐ it rusts the silverware.
☐ it comes with a warning from the
Surgeon General.

I'm learning a lot about survival here.
This week I learned:

☐ that screaming does not prevent
snakebite.
☐ that shoe leather can be very nutri-
tious.
☐ that if you're lost in the woods, it
doesn't help much to leave a trail of
bread crumbs.
☐ that there's nothing like a good flood

to make you forget about poison ivy.
The camp show is going to be great
this year, especially if:
- [ ] the police don't raid it.
- [ ] you like musicals based on the
  Franco-Prussian War.
- [ ] the mosquitoes don't eat the band.
- [ ] they can clear the skunks from the
  orchestra pit.

Next week is going to be really special
  because:
- [ ] they're taking down the quarantine
  signs.
- [ ] if the rain doesn't stop, we're going
  to learn how to mud-surf.
- [ ] we're borrowing a cow for riding
  lessons.
- [ ] we're going to untie our counselor.

Well, I've got to run along now. This is
  probably the last letter you'll receive
  from me at camp because:
- [ ] I've eaten all my stationery.
- [ ] I'm spending all my time digging an
  escape tunnel.
- [ ] the mailman refuses to come within
  ten miles of the camp.
- [ ] I've licked all the glue off my pos-
  tage stamps.
    - [ ] Best wishes,
    - [ ] With fond regrets,
    - [ ] Farewell forever,
    - [ ] Send help,

Visiting Day:
A Warning

Well, you made it halfway through the summer, and by this time, everyone knows you're a cool camper. But watch out—even the coolest campers can lose their cool in one quick day. We're talking, of course, about Visiting Day. Somehow, on Visiting Day parents know just what to do to embarrass you down to your sweat-socks.

To help you make it through this trying day, we've prepared a list of the awful, embarrassing things that are bound to happen. Show the list to your parents, and maybe—just maybe—they'll be able to resist doing a few of them.

This chapter is rated PG, Parental Guidance suggested. And if your parents are like most, they'll need all the guidance you can give them!

THINGS THAT WILL HAPPEN
ON VISITING DAY

1. Your mother will call you by your baby nickname ("Butterball") in front of your whole bunk!
2. Your father will show up in shorts and a camp T-shirt that's six sizes too small for him and loudly announce to everyone, "See, I look just like one of the campers now!"
3. Your mother will arrive with a broom and a mop and attempt to clean your bunk!
4. Your father will go up to the boy you've got a crush on and say, "You must be Susie's little boyfriend. She mentions you in every letter she writes!"
5. Instead of the treats you asked for, your parents will bring wheat germ and apples.
6. Your father will insist on making you and all your bunkmates pose for seven dozen photographs!
7. Your parents will jump up and yell "Bravo!" when you say your one line in the camp show.
8. Your parents will keep trying to pull the counselors aside and find out "how you're *really* doing."
9. Your father will get so excited, he'll jump and run over to join your side in the tug-of-war.

10. Your mother will announce in front of your entire bunk, "See—we told you you'd get over your homesickness. We didn't worry at all when you wrote that you cried yourself to sleep every night for a week!"

11. Your little brother will get stung by a bee and spend the entire weekend screaming.

12. Your parents will burst into tears and tell everyone, "Look at him! My little baby is so grown up now!"

The Cool Campers' Survival Kit

Most camps send out lists of what to bring to camp—such items as clothing, athletic supplies, and blankets. That list is complete enough for the average camper. But you're not going to be the average camper—you're going to be the cool camper, the one with the slight edge, the head start, that extra know-how! That's why our Survival Kit starts out with this important list.

TEN THINGS TO BRING TO CAMP
(That No One Ever Tells You to Bring)

1. An Almanac or Book of Facts and Records. Excellent for settling arguments: (Who hit more home runs—Willie Mays or Mickey Mantle?) *OR* for *starting* them: (Which city is farther west—Reno, Nevada, or Los Angeles, California? It's Reno. Look it up!)

2. Greeting Cards. If someone you care about has a birthday over the summer, better bring a card to send. A few of those funny "friendship" cards will also come in handy. Send them to your friends so they'll know you're still alive—when you don't have time to write.

3. Postcards. No, not the boring post-office kind. Take along a bunch of picture postcards from places you've been. Then send them to your friends during the summer. Won't they be surprised when they know you're at camp in Pennsylvania, and they get your card from the Grand Canyon!

4. Felt Markers, Plain White Paper, Cardboard, Scotch Tape, and Scissors. *No one* at camp ever has these items, even though they have a million different uses all summer. Tell your bunkmates that you've got this stuff, and watch how popular you get.

They're handy for fixing and labeling things. You'll also want to make signs for your bunk. "Hands off my Scotch tape!" might be a good one to start with!

5. One Special, Nice Outfit. Bring it along and don't wear it!

Somewhere along about the last week of camp, you're going to look as if you've been sleeping in your clothes for a month —and you probably will have been! What a thrill to have one super-nice, *clean* outfit to put on!

6. One Hand-Held Game. It can be the kind with the little silver balls that you have to line up. Or it can be one of those fancy electronic ones. Just be sure to bring one that you're really good at!

7. Extra Socks—All the Same Color. Camp

laundries eat socks, so it's a good idea to have extras. But what good is an extra pair of blue socks when you're missing a red one? Make it easier on yourself—bring all one color. (By the end of the summer you may actually have an even number!)

8. A Big Book of Riddles and Jokes. Take a joke book—please! It's the perfect aid for making rest period go faster. A good joke book can also be a lifesaver when your bunk can't think of anything to do for the annual talent show. Use the jokes to work up a comedy routine or skit.

9. A Few of Your Favorite Records. No, your bunk won't have a record player—but the Rec Hall probably will. And by the end of the summer everyone will be pretty sick of the same five records they've been hearing for months. That's when you appear with your prize collection of hits and heavies!

10. Something Wild and Crazy. If you or any member of your family has any one of the following items *bring it:*
a) a rhinestone tiara or crown
b) a rubber chicken or fish
c) hip-length boots
d) a mop top (that means just the cloth part—leave the handle at home)
e) any kind of mask

f) a huge (ten sizes too big for you) man's shirt

g) a fake mustache.

We know that none of these items appear on your camp supply list, and we wouldn't suggest *buying* any of them. But if you happen to have anything from this list lying around, you'll be amazed at how often it's just what's needed at camp—for shows, for jokes, for fun. Trust us. You'll use a fake mustache at least as often as you'll use your handy compass.

Now that you've added those ten necessities to your Must Bring list, here are—

FIVE THINGS *NOT* TO BRING TO CAMP

1. Do Not Bring Jigsaw Puzzles. We guarantee you'll lose three pieces before you even come close to finishing the puzzle.

2. Do Not Bring Favorite Books or Comics That You Don't Want To Lose. Bring only the books and comics you'll be glad to share and swap.

3. Do Not Bring Candy Bars. They'll melt in your trunk—not in your hand. Yeccch!

4. Do Not Bring Shirts with Lots of Buttons. Sure, your mom packed a sewing kit—but are you *really* going to sew on buttons? Stick to T-shirts and pull-overs.

5. Do Not Bring an Entire Drugstore with You. Leave those soaps, shampoos, suntan lotions, shoelaces, and combs at home. Chances are you'll be able to buy basic human necessities like these right in camp. You're not going off to the Sahara Desert, you know.

A TRICK FOR MOVIE NIGHT

Movie night at camp is always fun. The movies themselves aren't bad — but the real fun happens between the reels. For those few magic moments, the screen shines with a pure white light, the hall is dark, and a captive audience is ready — for what? For shadow animals, of course!

Luckily, you'll be ready, too. Let the others have their few seconds of glory with their quacky duck shadows and their bunny ears. Then get ready to knock them out with your fabulous version of — fanfare, please — a horse!

Practice at home until you can get your hands in the position you see in the

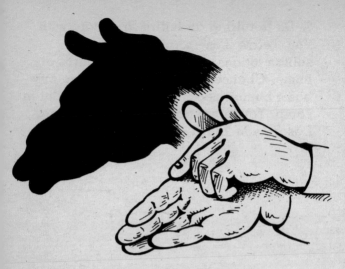

picture. Then you can make the horse neigh by separating the fingers that form the horse's muzzle.

Who's the camp shadow-animal champ? You're bound to be the whinnier!

AN AMAZING TRICK YOU CAN DO

We know you're a cool camper. And you know you're a cool camper — but the important thing is to let everyone else know you're a cool camper! One easy way to do this is to impress everyone with this amazing, mysterious, absolutely-guaranteed-to-work-every-time coin trick.

Here's the trick: You set three coins down on a piece of paper, all with heads up, and then turn your back, You tell someone to turn the coin over so that it's tails up. Then the person gets to switch the places of the coins as many times as he or she wants, before turning the chosen coin back to heads. Then — ta da! — you'll turn around and, even though all the coins are heads up, you'll be able to guess which coin had been turned over!

Sounds impossible, right? It's really very easy to learn. Here's what you do:

Use a nickel, a penny, and a dime. Now, take a piece of paper and write 1, 2, 3 across it in a row. Place the coins heads up on the paper under the numbers, just like in the picture below.

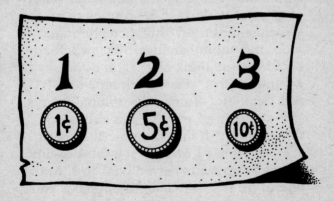

Be sure to put the dime under the three!

THREE is the key spot. The key spot is all that matters!

Okay, now turn your back. Tell your volunteers (it's best to do this in front of as large a group as possible) to turn over any one of the three coins so that it's tails up. Then tell them to switch the places of the two coins that were not turned over. Now the important part begins. Once they have done this, your friends can switch the places of any two coins as many times as they wish.

The only rule is that they have to tell you which coins they are switching. For example, a volunteer might say, "I'm switching Coin 2 and Coin 3. Now I'm switching 1 and 3. Now I'm switching 1 and 2." And so on.

Now, here's what you do: Remember we said that THREE is the key spot. What you've got to do is to keep track of all the switches that the THREE goes through.

So, if a volunteer says, "I'm switching 3 and 2," you think of 2. Then if the volunteer says, "I'm switching 2 and 1," you think of 1. If next, the volunteer says, "I'm switching 2 and 3," you still keep thinking of 1. If the volunteer then says, "I'm switching 1 and 3," you think about 3. Your key spot has moved back to 3. At the end of all the switches, the number you're thinking of is the key spot. Remember it!

After your volunteers have made all their switches, tell them to turn their chosen coin back to heads. Now, turn around and look at the coins. Look at your key spot. There are only two possibilities:

First Possibility: the dime will be on the key spot. If it *is*, the dime was the chosen coin.

Second Possibility: the dime *won't* be in the key spot. If it isn't, the dime is *not* the chosen coin — and neither is the coin that *is* in the key spot! That leaves only one other coin — the coin that isn't the dime and isn't in the key spot. That's the chosen coin.

Yes, we know this sounds very mysterious — but it works every time. Practice a few times and you'll be convinced. Just remember to keep careful track of what happens to that key spot.

This trick will last you all summer because the more times you do it, the more amazing it becomes. Don't be surprised if you're still demonstrating your amazing powers on the bus heading back home!

A GHOST STORY FOR YOU TO TELL

Okay, campers, gather around the campfire. Watch the last flickering embers of the fire fade into darkness. Feel the wind pick up. There isn't a sound now except for the soft crackle of the dying fire and the whisper and hum of the wind.

It's the perfect time for a good, old-fashioned, scare-the-socks-off-'em ghost story — and we've got a great one for you!

You'll be the greatest ghost-story teller at camp when you tell this tale of terror. Read it to yourself a few times so you can tell it or read it to everyone else — without scaring yourself to death!

We've even included a few directions on how to tell the story — directions that will add just the right creepy touch.

(Begin telling the story quietly and mysteriously.)

Once, not so many years ago, in a small town in an area very much like this one, there stood an old, old graveyard.

During the day, this graveyard looked pretty much like any other — rows of graves with plain white stones, a few sad old flowerbeds, and on the hill, a caretaker's shack. Just an ordinary graveyard.

But at night . . . at night . . . it was a very scary place. Some said it was haunted, and not just by the ghosts of the people buried there — but also by strange creatures, monsters that protected the graves by attacking anyone foolish enough to walk through the graveyard at night.

(Pause here briefly to give your listeners time to think about the graveyard monsters. Then continue, a little faster.)

Matt Douglas was the new kid in town. Maybe that's why when a bunch of kids dared him to go through the graveyard at midnight, he just had to accept the dare.

The date was chosen — Friday night.

Steve Myers was picked to take Matt to the graveyard gate to make sure he really went through with it.

"There's no such things as monsters and ghosts," Matt told himself all week, as the day drew closer and closer.

(Emphasize the days here.)

Tuesday! "There're no such things as monsters and ghosts."

Wednesday! "It's all just a silly story," Matt told himself.

Thursday! "There're no such things as monsters and ghosts."

Friday! "No such things as monsters and ghosts. No such things . . . no such things . . ." Matt whispered to himself as midnight drew closer.

"No such things as monsters and ghosts," he said again as Steve led him to the gate of the graveyard.

"Good luck," Steve whispered in a shaky voice.

Then, taking a deep breath, Matt was over the fence and inside.

(Pause here, Then resume telling the

*story quietly, slowly, and mysteriously,
with your voice nearly a whisper.)*

It was a dark night — only a tiny sliver
of moon to break the blackness. A chill
wind rustled the leaves on the gnarled old
trees. Slowly Matt started to make his way
through the paths between the dark, stony
graves.

(Scream this.) CRAAAAACK!

"Just a dry twig," Matt said aloud. Once
again he began to tell himself, "There're
no such things as monsters and ghosts. No
such things . . . "

(Tell this part very quietly.)

Matt could see the back gate now. All
he had to do was reach that gate, climb
the fence, and he'd win the dare.

The path grew darker, more twisted,
and the wind seemed to whisper and then
to howl, but Matt felt better now. Just a
few more steps.

"There're no such things as monsters
and ghosts. No such things . . . no such
things . . . . "

(Scream this as loud as you can.) "IT'S
GOT ME!!"

Something wet and coiled grabbed
Matt's ankles.

"LET GO! LET GO!" he screamed.

But each time he tried to get away, another slimy coil curled around his feet.

It was too dark. He couldn't see. He didn't know what slimy, hideous creature had hold on him.

"LET GO! LET GO!"

He screamed again and again. And then with all his effort, Matt pulled one foot free.

Suddenly, a sharp pain shot through his foot. He felt the creature's teeth through the thin soles of his sneakers. His foot throbbed, but the pain was nothing compared to the fear!

Then, in an instant, it was over.

Someone — or something — hit him hard on the forehead. And he went down and was out.

(Take a long pause here.)

And that's just where the caretaker found him the next morning. Bruised and unconscious, Matt made quite a weird sight.

His legs were still tangled up in the coils of the monster — the caretaker's garden hose.

And by his side lay the rake that had hit him in the head when he stepped on its sharp teeth!

All camps have their special songs.
Here's a very special one of your own.
Teach it to your bunkmates. It'll be music
to your ears — if to no one else's!

A CAMP SONG FOR YOUR BUNK

(Sung to the tune of "On Top of Old
Smokey")

On top of old rubbish
all covered with dust,
you'll find Bunk _____ (your number here),
a visit's a must.

Our bunk is the biggest,
biggest dump in the camp.
It may not be pretty,
but it's smelly and damp.

It's known at the neatest,
the cleanest one, too.
You've got to agree if
you're used to the zoo.

There's dust on the cupboards
and over your head.
But where can the clothes be?
Don't look under the bed!

We've got ants and spiders
all over our floors.
We don't like to brag, but
our bugs can beat yours!

Baseball and tennis —
all bunks can play these.
But try us at sleeping —
we'll win in a breeze.

We know you'll agree that
our bunk rates a ten,
'cause if you don't say so,
we'll sing this again!

(Repeat and keep repeating until no one in camp is speaking to anyone in your bunk.)

About the Authors

JOVIAL BOB STINE is an editor of humor magazines for children and has written more than forty books of humor and adventure for young people. He is married to JANE STINE, also a children's book author and head of her own company, which produces children's books. To get in the mood for this book, she pitched a tent (out of her apartment window) and sang camp songs until Bob was no longer jovial. They live and work in New York City with their son, Matthew.

About the Artist

JERRY ZIMMERMAN, a former truck driver, is married, has three children, and lives in Teaneck, New Jersey. Jerry loves to draw silly pictures—he giggles while he works! And he can draw everything from monsters to mashed potatoes.

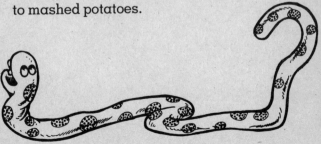